EMMANUEL JOSEPH

Nostalgia in the Machine Age, Solitude, Curiosity, and the Art of Staying Human

Copyright © 2025 by Emmanuel Joseph

All rights reserved. No part of this publication may be reproduced, stored or transmitted in any form or by any means, electronic, mechanical, photocopying, recording, scanning, or otherwise without written permission from the publisher. It is illegal to copy this book, post it to a website, or distribute it by any other means without permission.

First edition

This book was professionally typeset on Reedsy. Find out more at reedsy.com

Contents

1	Chapter 1: A Digital Dawn	1
2	Chapter 2: The Solitude of Screens	2
3	Chapter 3: Curiosity Unbound	3
4	Chapter 4: The Art of Human Connection	4
5	Chapter 5: The Quiet Revolution	5
6	Chapter 6: The Digital Renaissance	6
7	Chapter 7: The Ethics of Innovation	7
8	Chapter 8: The Future of Work	8
9	Chapter 9: The Digital Divide	9
10	Chapter 10: The Power of Play	10
11	Chapter 11: The Quest for Balance	11
12	Chapter 12: The Empathy Algorithm	12
13	Chapter 13: The Privacy Paradox	13
14	Chapter 14: The Resilience Factor	14
15	Chapter 15: The Innovation Imperative	15
16	Chapter 16: The Human Touch	16
17	Chapter 17: The Journey Forward	17

1

Chapter 1: A Digital Dawn

The dawn of the digital era brought with it waves of technological advancement. From the first computers to the rise of the internet, humans watched in awe as technology grew exponentially. Amidst the excitement, there was an undercurrent of nostalgia—a longing for simpler times when human connections were unmediated by screens. The beginning of the machine age marked a profound shift in the human experience.

As machines became more integrated into daily life, there were newfound conveniences but also growing concerns. People began to question the impact of technology on human relationships and personal identity. This chapter explores the dichotomy of progress and loss, examining how the digital dawn has reshaped the fabric of society.

Simultaneously, the chapter delves into the psychological impact of rapid technological changes. It discusses the paradox of feeling connected yet isolated, and the ways in which digital interactions differ fundamentally from face-to-face connections. The rise of social media and its influence on human behavior is also a focal point.

To encapsulate the essence of the digital dawn, personal anecdotes and historical milestones are interwoven, providing a rich narrative that captures both the excitement and apprehension of entering a new era. Through these stories, we understand the collective nostalgia that accompanies technological progress.

2

Chapter 2: The Solitude of Screens

The proliferation of screens in modern life has redefined solitude. Once considered a time for introspection and personal growth, solitude has taken on new meanings in the digital age. People now find themselves alone, yet constantly connected to a virtual world. This chapter explores the evolving nature of solitude in the context of technology.

From smartphones to tablets, screens have become portals to endless information and entertainment. However, this constant connectivity comes at a price. The chapter examines the psychological effects of screen-induced solitude, including the rise of digital addiction and the erosion of attention spans. It also highlights the impact on mental health and well-being.

In contrast, the chapter also presents the potential benefits of solitude in the digital age. It discusses how mindful use of technology can enhance personal growth and creativity. By setting boundaries and embracing moments of true solitude, individuals can find balance and reclaim the art of being alone.

Through a blend of scientific research and personal stories, the chapter paints a nuanced picture of solitude in the machine age. It underscores the importance of intentionality in navigating a world dominated by screens and advocates for a mindful approach to technology use.

3

Chapter 3: Curiosity Unbound

Curiosity has always been a driving force behind human innovation. In the machine age, curiosity takes on new dimensions as technology opens up previously unimaginable possibilities. This chapter delves into the ways in which curiosity has evolved alongside technological advancements and its impact on human exploration.

With access to vast amounts of information at our fingertips, curiosity has become more accessible than ever. The chapter explores the democratization of knowledge and how technology has empowered individuals to pursue their interests and passions. It highlights the role of online communities and digital platforms in fostering curiosity.

However, the chapter also addresses the challenges of navigating an information-saturated world. It discusses the importance of critical thinking and discernment in the face of misinformation and echo chambers. The need for a balanced approach to curiosity in the digital age is emphasized.

By weaving together historical examples and contemporary case studies, the chapter illustrates the enduring power of curiosity. It celebrates the human spirit of exploration and encourages readers to embrace their innate curiosity while remaining vigilant in the pursuit of truth.

4

Chapter 4: The Art of Human Connection

Despite the advances of the machine age, the art of human connection remains as vital as ever. This chapter examines the ways in which technology has both facilitated and hindered genuine human interactions. It explores the complexities of forming meaningful connections in a digital world.

From virtual friendships to online dating, technology has created new avenues for connection. The chapter discusses the benefits and drawbacks of these digital relationships, including the potential for superficial interactions and the impact on face-to-face communication skills. It also addresses the role of social media in shaping perceptions of connection.

In parallel, the chapter emphasizes the importance of preserving traditional forms of communication. It advocates for a balanced approach that incorporates both digital and in-person interactions. By nurturing face-to-face relationships, individuals can cultivate deeper connections and foster a sense of community.

Personal anecdotes and expert insights are woven throughout the chapter, offering a comprehensive understanding of the art of human connection. It encourages readers to prioritize genuine interactions and remain mindful of the impact of technology on their relationships.

5

Chapter 5: The Quiet Revolution

The machine age has sparked a quiet revolution in the way people seek solitude and quietude. This chapter explores the resurgence of interest in mindfulness, meditation, and other practices that promote inner peace. It examines the intersection of technology and tranquility.

As the world becomes increasingly noisy and fast-paced, there is a growing desire for moments of stillness. The chapter discusses the rise of digital detoxes and the movement towards unplugging from technology. It highlights the benefits of disconnecting and the ways in which individuals can create spaces for quiet reflection.

In addition, the chapter explores the role of technology in supporting mindfulness practices. From meditation apps to virtual retreats, technology can also be a tool for promoting inner peace. The key lies in finding a balance between connectivity and quietude.

Through stories of individuals who have embraced the quiet revolution, the chapter offers practical tips and inspiration for incorporating moments of tranquility into daily life. It emphasizes the importance of intentionality and the power of quietude in the machine age.

6

Chapter 6: The Digital Renaissance

The digital age has ushered in a renaissance of creativity and innovation. This chapter explores the ways in which technology has transformed the creative process and opened up new possibilities for artistic expression. It examines the intersection of art and technology in the modern era.

From digital art to virtual reality, technology has expanded the boundaries of what is possible in the creative realm. The chapter discusses the democratization of artistic tools and the rise of online platforms that enable creators to share their work with a global audience. It also highlights the impact of technology on traditional art forms.

However, the chapter also addresses the challenges faced by artists in the digital age. It discusses issues of copyright, digital piracy, and the pressure to constantly produce content. The need for a sustainable approach to creativity is emphasized.

By showcasing the stories of contemporary artists and innovators, the chapter celebrates the digital renaissance. It encourages readers to explore their own creative potential and embrace the possibilities offered by technology, while remaining mindful of the challenges.

7

Chapter 7: The Ethics of Innovation

As technology continues to evolve, ethical considerations become increasingly important. This chapter examines the ethical dilemmas and responsibilities that come with technological innovation. It explores the impact of technology on society and the importance of ethical decision-making.

From data privacy to artificial intelligence, the chapter discusses the key ethical issues facing the tech industry. It highlights the importance of transparency, accountability, and inclusivity in the development and deployment of new technologies. The role of regulation and public policy is also addressed.

In addition, the chapter explores the ethical responsibilities of individuals as users of technology. It discusses the need for digital literacy and critical thinking in navigating the digital landscape. The importance of ethical behavior in online interactions is emphasized.

Through case studies and expert insights, the chapter offers a comprehensive understanding of the ethics of innovation. It encourages readers to consider the broader implications of technology and to advocate for ethical practices in the digital age.

8

Chapter 8: The Future of Work

The machine age has transformed the world of work in profound ways. This chapter explores the impact of technology on employment and the changing nature of work. It examines the opportunities and challenges presented by automation, remote work, and the gig economy.

From artificial intelligence to robotics, technology has the potential to both displace and create jobs. The chapter discusses the implications of automation for different industries and the importance of reskilling and upskilling the workforce. It also highlights the role of technology in enabling remote work and flexible employment arrangements.

In addition, the chapter addresses the challenges faced by workers in the digital age. It discusses issues of job security, work-life balance, and the rise of the gig economy. The need for policies and practices that support workers in a changing landscape is emphasized.

Through stories of individuals navigating the future of work, the chapter offers practical insights and inspiration. It encourages readers to embrace the opportunities presented by technology while remaining mindful of the challenges and advocating for a fair and inclusive future of work.

9

Chapter 9: The Digital Divide

The machine age has brought about unprecedented connectivity, but it has also highlighted existing inequalities. This chapter explores the digital divide and its impact on different communities. It examines the barriers to access and the importance of digital inclusion.

From rural areas to underserved communities, the chapter discusses the challenges faced by those without reliable access to technology and the internet. It highlights the importance of infrastructure, affordability, and digital literacy in bridging the digital divide. The role of public and private sectors in addressing these issues is also addressed.

In addition, the chapter explores the social and economic implications of the digital divide. It discusses the impact on education, employment, and access to information and services. The importance of inclusive policies and practices is emphasized.

Through stories of individuals and communities working to bridge the digital divide, the chapter offers insights and inspiration. It encourages readers to advocate for digital inclusion and to recognize the importance of equitable access in the machine age.

Chapter 10: The Power of Play

Play is an essential aspect of the human experience, and the machine age has transformed the ways in which people engage in play. This chapter explores the role of play in personal growth, creativity, and social connection. It examines the impact of technology on play and the evolving nature of leisure.

From video games to virtual reality, technology has created new forms of play that offer immersive and interactive experiences. The chapter discusses the benefits of these digital games, including improved cognitive skills and social interactions. It also highlights the potential downsides, such as the risk of addiction and the impact on physical activity.

In parallel, the chapter emphasizes the importance of traditional forms of play. It advocates for a balanced approach that incorporates both digital and physical play. By engaging in a variety of playful activities, individuals can foster creativity, reduce stress, and enhance overall well-being.

Personal stories and expert insights are woven throughout the chapter, providing a comprehensive understanding of the power of play. It encourages readers to embrace their playful side and recognize the value of leisure in the machine age.

11

Chapter 11: The Quest for Balance

Finding balance in the digital age is a challenge faced by many. This chapter explores the pursuit of equilibrium between technology use and other aspects of life. It examines the impact of constant connectivity on work, relationships, and personal well-being.

The chapter discusses the concept of digital minimalism and the benefits of reducing screen time. It highlights strategies for achieving a healthy balance, such as setting boundaries, practicing mindfulness, and prioritizing offline activities. The importance of self-awareness and intentionality is emphasized.

In addition, the chapter addresses the role of technology in supporting work-life balance. From remote work to productivity apps, technology can be both a tool and a challenge in achieving equilibrium. The need for policies and practices that promote balance in the workplace is also discussed.

Through real-life examples and practical tips, the chapter offers insights and inspiration for finding balance in the machine age. It encourages readers to take a proactive approach to managing their relationship with technology and to prioritize their well-being.

12

Chapter 12: The Empathy Algorithm

Empathy is a fundamental human trait that enables connection and understanding. This chapter explores the role of empathy in the machine age and the ways in which technology can both enhance and hinder empathetic behavior.

The chapter discusses the rise of artificial intelligence and its potential to simulate empathy. It highlights the ethical implications of AI-driven interactions and the importance of maintaining genuine human connections. The role of technology in fostering empathy through virtual reality and online communities is also explored.

In contrast, the chapter addresses the challenges of cultivating empathy in a digital world. It discusses the impact of screen-mediated communication on emotional understanding and the potential for dehumanization in online interactions. The need for digital literacy and empathy education is emphasized.

By weaving together scientific research and personal anecdotes, the chapter provides a nuanced understanding of empathy in the machine age. It encourages readers to cultivate empathy in their daily lives and to harness the power of technology for positive social impact.

13

Chapter 13: The Privacy Paradox

The machine age has brought about unprecedented access to information, but it has also raised concerns about privacy. This chapter explores the privacy paradox and the challenges of navigating a world where personal data is constantly collected and shared.

The chapter discusses the ways in which technology has reshaped the concept of privacy. It highlights the benefits of data-driven services and the trade-offs involved in sharing personal information. The role of surveillance, data breaches, and the importance of cybersecurity are also addressed.

In addition, the chapter explores the psychological impact of living in a surveillance society. It discusses the ways in which privacy concerns can affect behavior and the importance of maintaining a sense of control over personal information. The need for digital literacy and informed consent is emphasized.

Through case studies and expert insights, the chapter provides a comprehensive understanding of the privacy paradox. It encourages readers to take a proactive approach to protecting their privacy and to advocate for policies that prioritize data security and user rights.

14

Chapter 14: The Resilience Factor

Resilience is the ability to adapt and thrive in the face of challenges, and it is a crucial trait in the machine age. This chapter explores the concept of resilience and the ways in which technology can both support and undermine it.

The chapter discusses the impact of digital stressors, such as information overload and social comparison, on mental health and well-being. It highlights strategies for building resilience, including mindfulness, self-care, and digital detoxes. The importance of community support and social connections is also emphasized.

In parallel, the chapter explores the role of technology in promoting resilience. From mental health apps to online support groups, technology can provide valuable resources for coping with stress and adversity. The need for a balanced approach to technology use is emphasized.

Through personal stories and expert insights, the chapter offers practical tips and inspiration for cultivating resilience in the machine age. It encourages readers to embrace challenges as opportunities for growth and to harness the power of technology for positive change.

15

Chapter 15: The Innovation Imperative

Innovation is a driving force behind technological progress, and it is essential for addressing the challenges of the machine age. This chapter explores the importance of innovation and the ways in which individuals and organizations can foster a culture of creativity and experimentation.

The chapter discusses the key factors that drive innovation, including curiosity, risk-taking, and collaboration. It highlights the role of technology in enabling new forms of innovation and the importance of a supportive environment. The need for diversity and inclusivity in the innovation process is also emphasized.

In addition, the chapter addresses the challenges of sustaining innovation in a rapidly changing world. It discusses the importance of adaptability, continuous learning, and resilience. The role of leadership in fostering a culture of innovation is also explored.

Through case studies and real-life examples, the chapter provides insights and inspiration for embracing the innovation imperative. It encourages readers to cultivate a mindset of curiosity and experimentation and to contribute to a future that is both innovative and inclusive.

16

Chapter 16: The Human Touch

Amidst the advancements of the machine age, the human touch remains irreplaceable. This chapter explores the importance of maintaining human qualities, such as empathy, creativity, and compassion, in a technology-driven world.

The chapter discusses the ways in which technology can enhance, but never replace, the human touch. It highlights the importance of human-centered design and the need for technology that supports, rather than diminishes, human qualities. The role of education and lifelong learning in cultivating these qualities is also emphasized.

In parallel, the chapter addresses the challenges of preserving the human touch in a digital world. It discusses the impact of screen-mediated communication on empathy and emotional understanding, and the importance of face-to-face interactions. The need for a balanced approach to technology use is emphasized.

Through personal stories and expert insights, the chapter provides a comprehensive understanding of the human touch in the machine age. It encourages readers to prioritize human qualities and to harness the power of technology for positive social impact.

17

Chapter 17: The Journey Forward

As the machine age continues to evolve, the journey forward is one of constant adaptation and growth. This chapter explores the ways in which individuals and society can navigate the challenges and opportunities of the digital age with resilience, curiosity, and humanity.

The chapter discusses the importance of lifelong learning and adaptability in a rapidly changing world. It highlights the role of education and self-directed learning in preparing for the future. The need for a proactive approach to personal and professional development is emphasized.

In addition, the chapter explores the ways in which technology can support a positive future. From innovation in healthcare to sustainable development, technology has the potential to address some of the world's most pressing challenges. The importance of ethical and inclusive practices is also emphasized.

Through stories of individuals and communities embracing the journey forward, the chapter offers inspiration and practical insights. It encourages readers to approach the future with optimism and a sense of possibility, and to contribute to a world that is both technologically advanced and deeply human.

In an era where technology reigns supreme, "**Nostalgia in the Machine Age: Solitude, Curiosity, and the Art of Staying Human**" is a poignant exploration of the human experience amidst the digital revolution. Through seventeen insightful chapters, this book delves into the intricate relationship between humanity and technology, shedding light on the nostalgia that accompanies progress.

From the dawn of the digital age to the complexities of maintaining genuine connections in a world dominated by screens, each chapter offers a profound examination of the ways in which technology has reshaped our lives. Discover the evolving nature of solitude, the boundless potential of curiosity, and the delicate balance required to navigate a world of constant connectivity.

With a blend of scientific research, personal anecdotes, and expert insights, this book addresses the ethical dilemmas, mental health challenges, and societal impacts of living in the machine age. It advocates for a mindful and intentional approach to technology use, emphasizing the importance of preserving the human touch, fostering creativity, and cultivating empathy.

"Nostalgia in the Machine Age" is not just a reflection on the past; it is a guide for the future. It encourages readers to embrace the journey forward with resilience, curiosity, and a commitment to staying human in an ever-evolving digital landscape.

www.ingramcontent.com/pod-product-compliance
Lightning Source LLC
LaVergne TN
LVHW020509080526
838202LV00057B/6260